Red

Written by Josephine Selwyn

Picture Dictionary

chilli pepper

flower

notebook

Read the picture dictionary. You will find these words in the book.

strawberry

tomato

wheelbarrow

Look at the flower.
It is a red flower.

petal

Look at the notebook.
It is a red notebook.

cover

Look at the tomato.
It is a red tomato.

skin

Look at the wheelbarrow.
It is a red wheelbarrow.

tray

Look at the chilli pepper.
It is a red chilli pepper.

pod

Look at the strawberry.
It is a red strawberry.

fruit

Activity Page

1. Use red construction blocks to make a red vehicle.

2. Use cardboard to make a red stop sign.

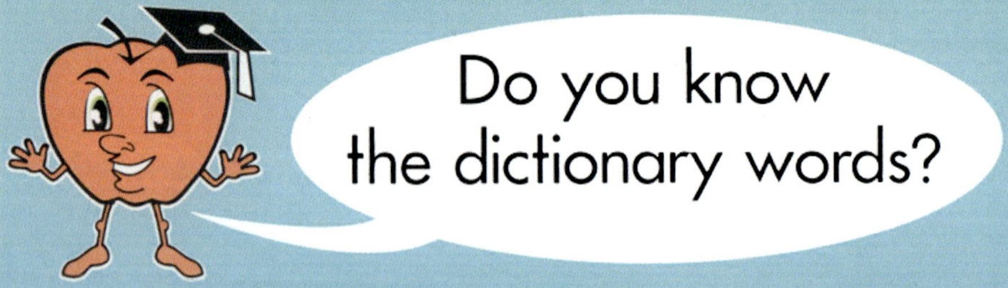